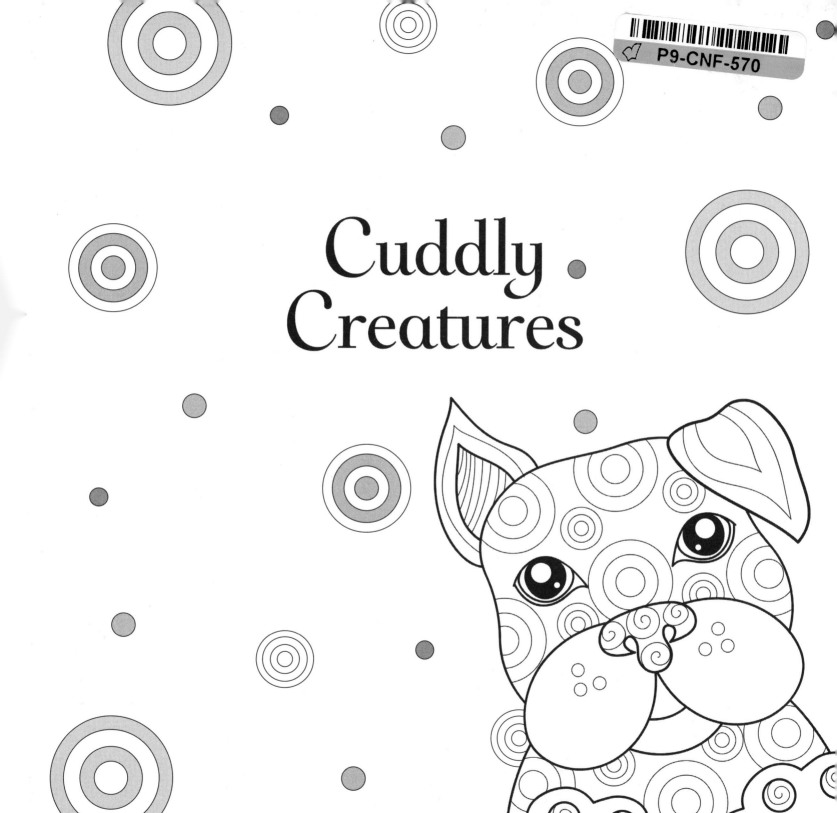

Cuddly Creatures

ZENDOODLE COLORSCAPES: CUDDLY CREATURES.
Copyright © 2019 by St. Martin's Press. All rights reserved.
Printed in Canada. For information, address
St. Martin's Press, 175 Fifth Avenue, New York, N.Y. 10010.

www.stmartins.com
www.castlepointbooks.com

The Castle Point Books trademark is owned by Castle Point Publishing, LLC.
Castle Point books are published and distributed by St. Martin's Press.

ISBN 978-1-250-23038-6 (trade paperback)

Our books may be purchased in bulk for promotional, educational, or business use.
Please contact your local bookseller or the Macmillan Corporate and Premium
Sales Department at 1-800-221-7945, extension 5442, or by e-mail
at MacmillanSpecialMarkets@macmillan.com.

First Edition: May 2019

10 9 8 7 6 5 4 3 2 1

zendoodle colorscapes

Cuddly Creatures

Baby Animals
to Color and Display

Featuring
artwork by
Jeanette Wummel,
Deborah Muller,
and **Jodi Best**

CASTLE POINT BOOKS
NEW YORK

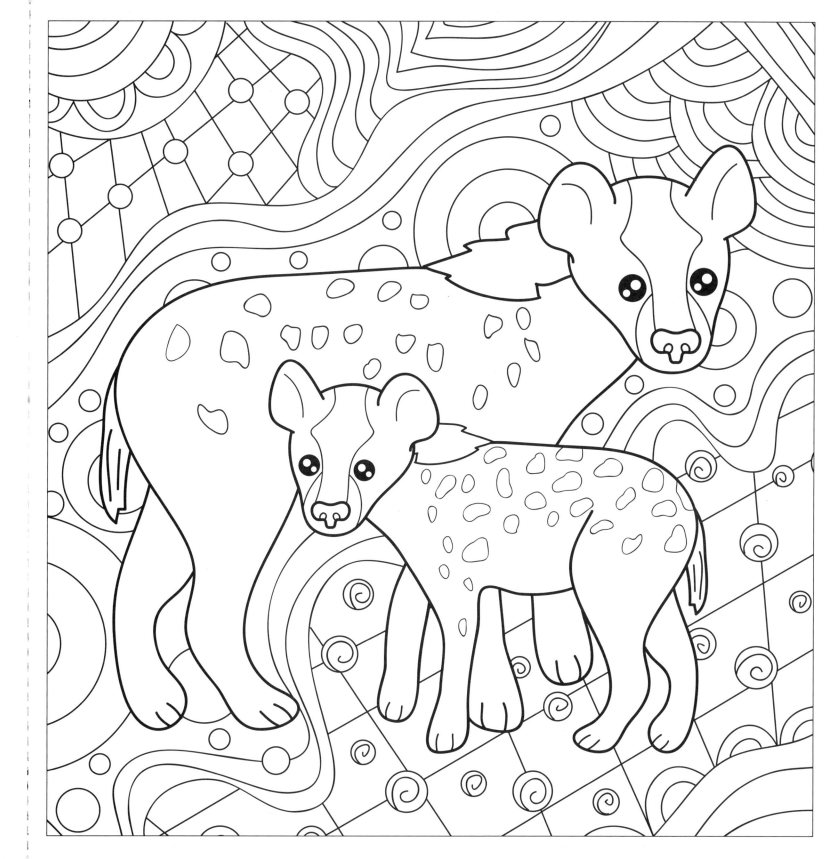

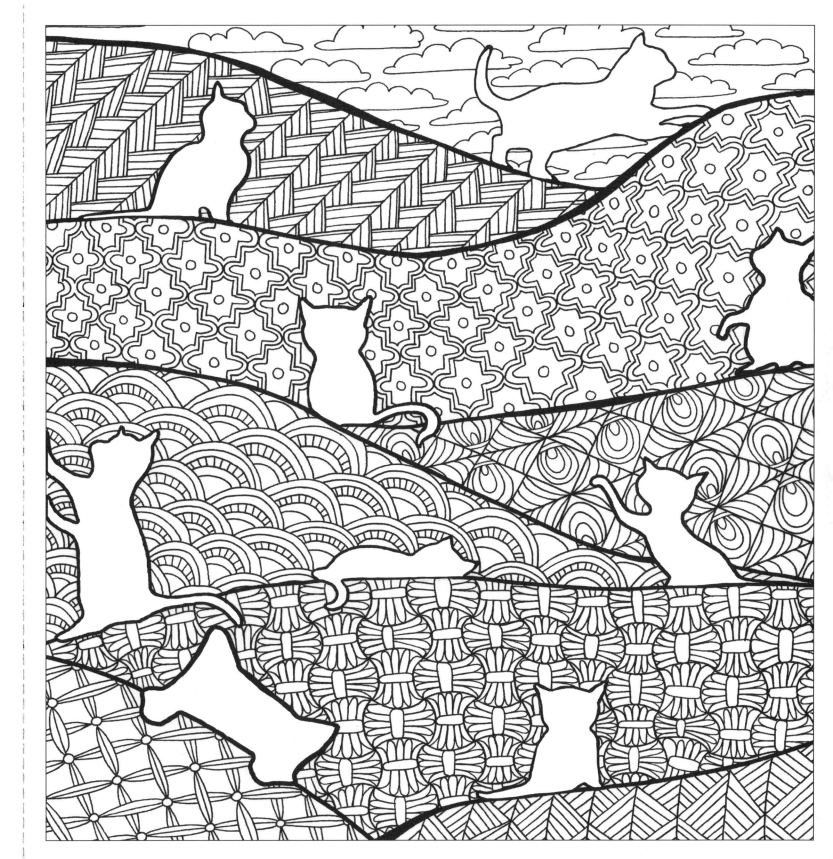

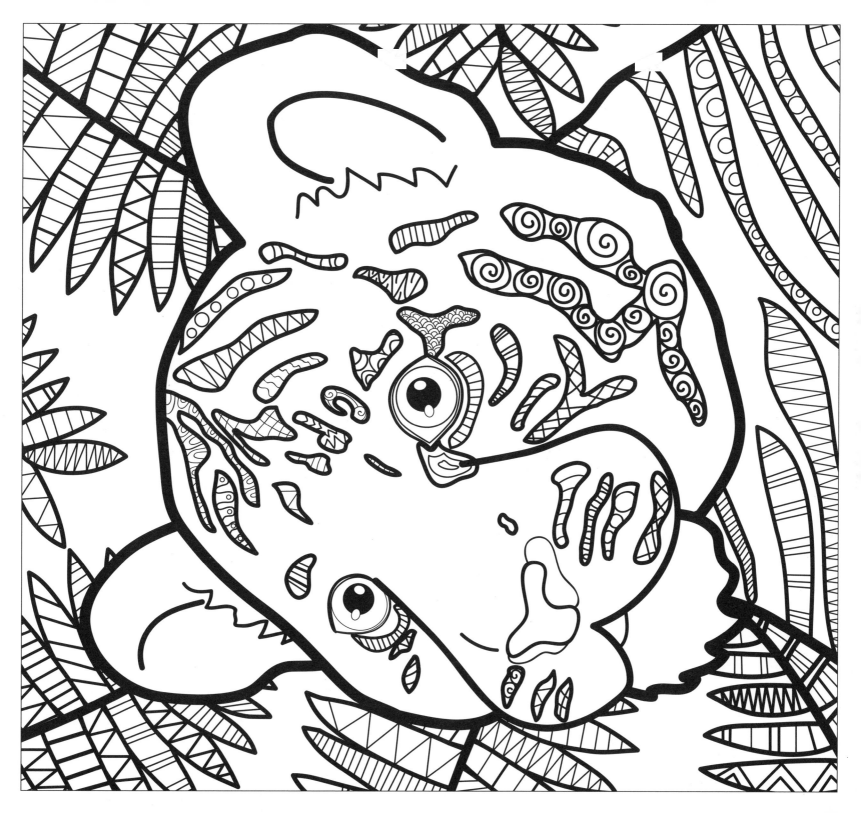